Woodworking for Beginners

A Guide for Teaching Beginners About Basics of Woodworking and About Using the Right Tools in a Right Way To Achieve Success with Woodworking Projects

By Daren Rodney

© **Copyright 2019 - All rights reserved.**

The content contained within this book may not be reproduced, duplicated or transmitted without direct written permission from the author or the publisher.

Under no circumstances will any blame or legal responsibility be held against the publisher or author for any damages, reparation, or monetary loss due to the information contained within this book. Either directly or indirectly.

Legal Notice:

This book is copyright protected. This book is only for personal use. You cannot amend, distribute, sell, use, quote or paraphrase any part, or the content within this book, without the consent of the author or publisher.

Disclaimer Notice:

Please note the information contained within this document is for educational and entertainment purposes only. All effort has been executed to present accurate, up to date and reliable, complete information. No warranties of any kind are declared or implied. Readers acknowledge that the author is not engaging in the rendering of legal, financial, medical or professional advice. The content within this book has been derived from various sources. Please consult a licensed professional before attempting any techniques outlined in this book.

By reading this document, the reader agrees that under no

circumstances is the author responsible for any losses, direct or indirect, which are incurred as a result of the use of information contained within this document, including, but not limited to, —errors, omissions, or inaccuracies.

Contents

Introduction To Woodworking 1

Chapter 1: Protection First...4

    Health Concerns..8

Chapter 2: Hardwoods Vs Softwoods..11

    Typical Misconceptions..12

    Choosing What to Utilize 13

Chapter 3: Different Saws Styles..18

    Picking the Right Saw Blade...18

    Quantity of Teeth 19

    Gullet 20

    The Hook Angle..20

    Tooth Setups 21

    Hand Saws 22

Chapter 4: Measure Two Times, Cut One Time. 23

    Rules and Tape Measures 24

    Squares and T-Bevels 26

    Marking Tools 28

Chapter 5: Chisel Essentials. 29

    Utilizing Your Chisel...30

    Sharpening..31

Chapter 6: Selecting Hand Tools. 33

Chapter 7: Adhesives 38

    Polyvinyl Acetates 39

    Resorcinol and Urea-Formaldehyde 40

  Epoxy 42

Chapter 8: Sharpening Tools...43
  Oilstones..44
  Waterstones 44
  Diamond Stones 45
  Metal Lapping Plates 45

Chapter 9: Making Joints 47
  Square-Ended Butt Joints...47
  Mitered Butt Joint 47
  Edge-to-Edge Butt Joint 48
  Tongue and Groove Joint..48
  Doweled Frame Joints...49
  Edge-to-Edge Dowel Joint...49
  Carcass Butt Joints 49
  Corner Bridle Joint 50
  Mitered Bridle Joint 50
  T-Bridle Joint 50
  Lap Joint 51
  Through Mortise and Tenon Joint...51

Chapter 10: Choosing What To Construct 52

Chapter 11: Developing Working Drawings...57
  Preparing Fundamentals 59

Chapter 12: Fillers and Finishes..61
  Oils 61
  Urethane and Varnish 63
  Oil/Varnish Mixes..64

Wax 65

Wiping Varnishes 65

Shellac 66

Lacquers 66

Fillers 67

Thank you for buying this book and I hope that you will find it useful. If you will want to share your thoughts on this book, you can do so by leaving a review on the Amazon page, it helps me out a lot.

Introduction To Woodworking

Woodworking includes a multitude of varied activities, consisting of woodcarving, turning, cabinet making, marquetry and joinery, nevertheless, every expert craftspersonhas at some point learned the basics of determining and marking, dimensioning, putting together and completing which are looked at the fundamentals of woodworking abilities which are the root of any woodworking undertaking.

The capability to think in 3 dimensions is required to define the wood for a task and to envision how one element fits with the other and what order is needed of a woodworker. You are going to additionally require to understand which tools are going to provide the most effective outcomes, depending upon the level of precision needed and the characteristics of the wood you are utilizing.

Dimensioning is the procedure of minimizing basic materials precisely to size. This nearly inevitably requires planning with components-- a procedure that is easy in concept, however, it takes a great deal of practice to end up being excellent.

Cutting and putting together a range of joints are part of all but the most basic of woodworking ventures. Long considered as a measure of a woodworker's abilities, joinery requires a consistent hand-eye coordination, however the experience is going to inform you of the ideal method to attach one piece of wood to another magnificently and inconspicuously without compromising strength.

One needed addition to these critical abilities is an admiration of how wood acts. It is a special, living material which continues to bulge and compress with humidity changes, an element that a woodworker needs to deal within the design of every undertaking. Cerain woods are simpler to deal with than others, and every piece is distinctive in the way the grain twists and turns.

There is no single best method to perform anything in woodworking. The ideal way is the way that works ideally for you and what works most effectively is a balance between the time something requires, the tools offered, the enjoyment you have from the procedure and the quality of outcomes you are searching for.

There are points for both the utilizitaion of hand tools and the utilization of devices for woodworking. Some state that utilizing hand tools enables you to establish the 'propensity' of cutting and forming wood without grain tearing. While other woodworking specialists declare that you could frequently finish a task in less time using hand tools as a result of the setup needed for the mechanical tools. Others think simply the opposite. We are going to go over both choices, machine and hand tools within this guide.

With a bit of perseverance, the ideal tool and methods and a great set of strategies, you do not need to be Bob Villa to construct something you are going to value for many years to come.

Chapter 1: Protection First

Any conversation of woodworking equipment must start with store safety; hand tools need safety measures too. Woodworking devices are created to cut, slice, abrade, cut, drill and shave components which are substantially tougher than human skin. When utilized thoughtlessly, devices are harmful and when utilized effectively, devices can be a fantastic assistance.

Wherever woodworkers congregate, stories of mishaps and near-misses turn up eventually. Maybe the word 'accident' is misguiding here due to the fact that 'accident' indicates the hurt individual is a 'victim' of circumstances outside their control; most of the times, it might be more suitable to state that the 'perpetrator' suffers the repercussions of his/her own negligence.

The awareness of safety is the primary necessity of great workmanship. Here are numerous things you may do to secure yourself while dealing with wood, either with hand tools or machines.

Use eye and hearing protection when utilizing routers, saws, sanders and other devices. To maintain dust and splinters out of your eyes, utilize big plastic protection goggles, safety glasses and a face shield.

1. Safety glasses-- the stiff safety goggles lenses are encompassed by a soft plastic frame which suits and seals versus the curves of your face. The sides are aerated to stop condensation and they could be placed across prescription glasses.

2. Hearing protectors-- cushioned ear muffs and earplugs shield your hearing from too much exposure to the commotion. Constantly use protectors when utilizing loud power tools that might cause long-lasting harm to your hearing.

Keep your workshop location tidy and orderly so you will not trip over a wood scrap or an extension cable at a troublesome moment.

Tie long hair up; do not use loose-fitting clothes or any accessories. All of these products could get captured in the devices and draw you in the direction of the blades or other pointy sections.

Do not utilize equipment when you are exhausted or have actually consumed alcohol. Any quantity of alcohol, even a bit is excessive for running machinery. This kind of equipment is harmful enough when you are completely alert, so why raise the possibilities of something bad happening?

Concentrate on what you are doing constantly and relax if your mind begins to stray. You are more than likely to suffer an accident when carrying out the identical operation repeatedly. Leave for a couple of minutes in between cuts.

If you are not comfy making a cut or aren't certain if a specific cut is safe, get suggestions or assistance prior to trying it. Discover a friendly woodworker to ask, maybe at the neighborhood high school or university.

Maintain saw blades sharp. The more you need to press, the less command you with the wood. This could result in slips and loss of fingers or even worse.

Be ready for accidents. Think about these things:

1. Where is your phone?

2. Where is your first aid set?-- You must constantly have a comprehensive first aid set readily handy constantly.

3. Where is the closest individual who can aid you?-- You must never ever be on your own while woodworking.

4. Can you provide clear instructions to your shop using the phone?

5. Are you knowledgeable about standard tourniquet and first-aid methods?

If a major accident does take place, contact 911, not your buddy. Your buddy is not going to have the ability to assist you if you all of a sudden enter into shock en route to the hospital.

If you are so unlucky to sever any fingers, take them with you to the medical facility in the event they are able to be reattached. Severed fingers need to be covered in gauze and immersed in a cup of salted water which is maintained cold in ice; the fingers must never touch the ice.

Health Concerns

Breathing sawdust is not good; it could be allergenic, poisonous and carcinogenic. The sawdust from certain imported woods, involving teak, is especially damaging and is understood to trigger skin rashes and repertory issues. Numerous research studies have actually revealed that woodworkers have an elevated nasal cancer rate.

Due to the fact that even a bit of sawdust is able to block sinuses and exacerbate allergic reactions, attempt to use a mask whenever you make dust, whether it is from sandpaper or equipment or sweeping the flooring. Masks vary from the thick rubber with a disposable toxic-fume-proof filter to thin paper with a flexible strap. The heavy-duty masks are normally uncomfortable to use so some compromise is going to have to be made between effectiveness and convenience.

A few of the finishes and solvents utilized in finishing furniture are likewise allergenic, carcinogenic and poisonous. Petroleum distillates in commercial oil finishes, benzene and naphtha are all possible contaminants. Due to the fact that a number of these solvents are poisonous to the body by respiration or through skin contact, it's a great idea to use a toxic-vapor mask and rubber gloves when dealing with them.

Woodshop accidents take place in a flash, particularly with power tools. The outcomes could be permanent and even deadly. Your initial line of defense versus accidents is truly straightforward; Think before performing. Respect the abilities and risks of your tools and know how to utilize them properly.

Plan your work so you are able to get assistance moving or lifting heavy things. Set high requirements for tool upkeep and operations. Never

ever utilize dull bits or blades. Get rid of guards and other protection devices only when definitely required. And keep your work area clear of clutter and mess.

Chapter 2: Hardwoods Vs Softwoods.

Lumber could be organized into 2 broad classifications-- hardwoods and softwoods -- based upon a botanical distinction. Hardwoods are those types that originate from leaf-bearing trees which generate fruits, flowers, or nuts. Typical North American hardwood lumber consists of oak, maple, walnut, ash, cherry, birch, beech and poplar.

There are lots of less prevalent Western hardwoods too, such as butternut, holly, mesquite, sycamore and pear. Other nations log many hardwood species too. A few of these exotics consist of teak, ebony, mahogany, bubinga, rosewood, pear and purpleheart. These exotic woods could be bought via the Web or specialized brochures; nevertheless, they are expensive and might just be available in a constrained size.

Softwoods originate from the big cone-bearing tree family which bears needles instead of leaves. Pines and firs of all kinds, redwood, cypress and cedar are generally North American softwoods formed into board lumber. Since these types are well fit for building functions, all lumber utilized for framing and roughing construction originates from softwood trees.

They are adequately sturdy for structural uses, yet are simple to operate with typical power or hand tools. Another benefit is that cone-bearing trees proliferate and establish straighter branches and trunks than the hardwoods. And lastly, more softwood trees could be sown per acre than hardwood trees so they generate a greater lumber yield quicker.

Typical Misconceptions

It is a typical misconception that hardwoods are referred to as hardwood since the wood is hard, while softwood is called so since they are soft. It holds true that lots of hardwoods are harder than softwoods, nevertheless, the difference, in fact, has nothing to do with the workability or solidity.

Southern yellow pine, for instance, is heavy thick softwood utilized for stair treads and big framing lumber. It accepts fasteners in a way such as that of hardwoods. Poplar and walnut are frequent hardwoods, however, they could be sawn and routed as quickly as redwood or cedar.

Even pricing is not a great sign of softwoods or hardwoods. More softwood is produced into building components than furniture-grade lumber, however, what does end up being lumber could be rather costly. Take, for example, clear sugar pine lumber, it is equally as pricey as white oak or premium cherry.

In fact, the fundamental economics of demand and supply have more to do with lumber prices than the specific wood species or perhaps its grade classification.

Choosing What to Utilize

Woodworking ventures can utilize both hardwoods and softwoods. Usually, hardwoods wind up as indoor tasks such as trim-work, furniture, cabinets and turnings since the wood figures and grain are extremely desirable. Softwoods have a tendency to end up being outdoor furniture, kids' projects like tree houses and other kinds of utility or painting undertakings. These are simply basic instructions. If cash is no object, you could develop kids' furniture from almost any furniture-grade lumber you possess.

The responses to what kinds to pick for a specific venture are not cut and dry.

Ask yourself a couple of questions.

Is this an interior or exterior undertaking? The majority of wood is going to deteriorate gradually in the existence of ultraviolet sunlight or water. Wetness is another 'fatal' hazard to wood; it welcomes wood and mold-boring pests. A few of the most resilient outdoor woods consist of cypress, western red cedar, redwood and white oak. These lumbers consist of natural oils or profiling substances that withstand rot and aid to ward off pests. Boatbuilding woods like teak and mahogany are outstanding options, even though they are far more pricey than the typical weather-resistant varieties.

Think about utilizing a pressure-treated wood in case you are not utilizing it for food or contact with skin (like a bench or chair). It accepts paint effectively when the infused chemicals dry and the wood has a tendency to be required for years. Take care and use a dust respirator when machining pressure-treated lumber to avoid breathing in the sawdust, which includes the bad chemicals.

Is the venture going to be painted or get a clear finish? For painted ventures, select the wood with a soft texture without a hefty grain pattern. Preferably, the lumber must finish and sand so efficiently that the grain totally vanishes. Excellent paint-grade hardwoods consist of birch, birch and aspen. These likewise have a tendency to be more economical than woods with more appealing wood grain patterns. Softwoods normally create a blotchy, irregular tone when they are finished using a stain, however they make outstanding affordable painted woods. Firs, pines, and other 'white woods' are great prospects for paint finishes.

What density and percentages of lumber does your venture need? Almost all the board lumber you are going to discover in a lumberyard or a home center is going to be grated to 3/4- inch density. There could be a percentage of 'craft' woods in 1/4- inch density made from poplar or oak along with laminated blanks in a couple of sizes up to 3 inches thick. Lengths of 'craft' woods are going to be restricted to about 3 feet. Some ventures need big panels like entertainment centers and tables and if you do not own clamp and a jointer to glue your own broad panels from narrower boards, your neighborhood home shop most likely keeps sanded pre-glued panels as broad as 3 feet and up to 8 feet long.

Which venture parts are going to show? Frequently practiced in furniture building is to utilize secondary or less expensive lumber on the interiors and rears of pieces and the more pricey, better wood on the external regions of the furniture. Places where secondary wood may be utilized for are drawers, racks Within a cabinet, the rears of desks and cabinets, beneath the tabletop, legs, and so on. Pine and poplar are frequently incorporated into ventures as secondary wood pieces.

What does your budget plan permit? Lumber is pricey, especially if you purchase it entirely surfaced. In some cases sticker shock is going to press you over the edge and make your lumber choice apparent. When tallying up the quantity of lumber you are going to want to factor in another 20 to 30 percent extra wood. The excess usually gets utilized in the end. If the cost is out of reach, think about utilizing a more cost-effective wood and staining it to suit the color of more costly wood.

Chapter 3: Different Saws Styles

There are numerous things to think about when selecting a saw blade-- ensuring, sleek cuts using your radial arm saw, table saw; chop saw or compound slider miter saw depends upon having the appropriate blade for the tool and, for the type of cut you want to make. Effectiveness differs from one blade to another and currently, there is not an absence of them in the shops today, so pick intelligently.

Picking the Right Saw Blade

It's not all that convoluted, truly. So as to assemble a top-rate saw blade array of your own, you needed to determine a tiny amount regarding what diverse blades do and what differentiates the high-quality from the more affordable ones. As soon as you figure this out, you'll have the ability to choose the blade that is finest for the kind of woodworking you are going to be doing.

There are blades which are meant to do a variety of things. Several blades are for ripping wood, crosscutting wood, slicing plywood and veneered panels, slicing melamine, slicing non-ferries metals and slicing laminates and plastics. General-purpose and combination blades, these blades are for utilizing two or more types of cuts. The quantity of teeth, the hook angles, the gullet and the tooth setup all determine how excellent the saw blade is.

Quantity of Teeth

Saw blades with less teeth move the wood quicker. Additionally, blades with more teeth provide a smoother cut. For instance, a 10' blade for ripping wood normally has less than 25 teeth and is meant to move the thing rapidly through the device along the grain extent. With the least amount of work and leaving a fresh cut, the higher quality rip blade is going to surpass a lower quality one that is not created for mirror-like effortless cuts.

Conversely, a crosscut blade is well made to provide you an even cut crossways versus the wood grain with no splintering or tearing. Between 60 and 80 teeth are located on the crosscut blade. Keep in mind, moving less material, every tooth get in less contact with the wood and this implies that a crosscut sharp edge makes countless extra smoother and single cuts when compared to the ripping blades. A refined finish is going to show up on the wood if utilizing a top quality crosscut cutting edge.

Gullet

The area missing from the blade plate ahead of every tooth, that enables chip extraction, is referred to as the gullet. In the crosscutting blade, the chips are tinier and fewer per tooth so the gullet is a lot tinier. In the ripping blades the pace is a lot quicker than the crosscutting action and the chips are larger so for that reason the gullet has to be larger to support the bigger quantity of components coming through it.

The Hook Angle

Instead of being completely in accordance with the blade, the teeth are pointed either outward or inward, depending upon the blade setup. Hook angle is the slant shaped linking a tooth face and a line drawn down the blade middle throughout the tooth tip. A downbeat angle of the hook symbolizes the teeth tip far from the course of rotary movement and the reverse is stated for the positive hook angle. A zero hook slant shows the teeth remain in line with the blade center.

A really aggressive hook angle (20 or more degrees) is going to likewise have a really quick cutting rate. A low hook or negative setting is going to have a slower supply pace and is going to prevent the blade from 'climbing up' the material as it frequently does.

Tooth Setups

The way the blade slices is typically impacted by the way the tooth is formed and the way they are organized together. The setup pertains to the way a blade is going to cut, in case it's a ripper, crosscutting or laminates cutter.

Hand Saws

Nobody can refute the aggressive pace of a sliding chopsaw or a table saw, nevertheless, for joinery, it's difficult to trump the backsaw's accuracy for slicing only what you require. Hand saws are more affordable and simpler to manage than machine saws. The backsaw is able to hold the thinnest, sharpest of blades and they are able to slice wood with minimal waste and utmost control.

Chapter 4: Measure Two Times, Cut One Time.

A lot of woodworkers do not provide much thought to the majority of standard tools in their store, they are too hectic choosing the most effective scrapers, chisels, clamps, exclusive jigs, hand planes, tools, woodworking equipment, and all manner of add-ons to make their work go efficiently and more precisely. What they are missing out on is the marking and measuring instruments.

Take a look at what you have in the way of marking and measuring instruments. A lot of the regular problems in woodworking are out of a four-sided figure frames, joints, casework that suit improperly, etc. and they could be traced back to the marking and measuring errors. The perpetrator is typically just a question of using the inaccurate measuring and marking instrument for the task. A tape measure was not determined for the exceptionally precise measurements that a lot of woodworking tasks need.

In the majority of woodworking tasks, the initial thing you to do is measuring and marking linear measurements. Miscalculations as tiny as 100th of an inch when measuring and marking in such complex joinery or little, firm parts are going to, later on, appear as spaces in joints or irregular parts or a slew of other less-than-ideal outcomes.

Depending upon to what extent you do have the ability to interpret a measurement into an unbiased mark on a piece of wood is the result of measuring from point 1 to point 2. Holding down a measuring tape while attempting to mark off a measurement precisely is a struggle, generally, since measuring tapes are not meant to lay flat. A precisely adjusted and understandable marking and measuring instrument is required for all woodworking tasks.

Rules and Tape Measures

Given that even the most effective measuring tools are reasonably affordable, many woodworkers get a range of tape measures and rules to fulfill various requirements. Nevertheless, it is a good idea to utilize the exact same measuring tool or rule during the task, simply in case there is any variation in between one tool and the next. Buy both tape measures and rules with conventional and metric graduations-- however make sure not to puzzle one system with another when you have actually started to define a workpiece. You could measure a single piece of wood precisely and after that utilize it as a design template for the other pieces in case more than one of the identical size is required, this is going to conserve you time during the measuring and marking department.

1. Tape measure-- retractable steel tapes, going from 6 to 16 feet (2 to 5m) long, are normally graduated along both edges. A lock button stops the immediate retracting of the tape. Several tape measures integrate a liquid-crystal screen that informs you how far the tape had actually been pulled from the case; an integrated memory maintains the measurements when the tape is pulled back. Self-adhesive steel tapes are offered without cases for sticking along the leading workbench edge.

2. Four-fold rule-- The folding carpenter's rule created from boxwood with end capes and brass hinges is still prominent amongst conventional artists. A lot of folding rules are 3ft (1m) in length completely extended. Since it is reasonably dense,

you need to stand a wood rule on edge if you want to transfer measurements properly to the work. Comparable rules created from plastic are, in some cases, made with diagonal edges to get over this issue.

3. Straightedge-- each workshop requires at least one tough metal straightedge, being in between 1ft 8in and 6ft 6in long. A diagonal straight edge is perfect for precise cuts using a marking knife and for evaluating if a planed surface is completely flat. Certain straightedges are engraved with conventional metrics and/or graduations.

Squares and T-Bevels

Squares are utilized to ensure things are at an ideal angle to each other. In a woodshop, these things may be the tenon shoulder, the board edge, the jointer fence etc. Nevertheless, a square is an abstract word. Looked at carefully enough, absolutely nothing is really square; certain things simply approach the concept of being squarer than other things. There are 3 kinds of squares usually utilized in woodworking.

1. Try squares are the most typically utilized squares amongst makers of furniture. They feature blades of steel or brass (typically from 6in to 12in long) embeded in a thicker metal or wood stock. In case the stock is wood, it must be faced with metal to guarantee long-lasting precision. The dependability of try squares can differ dramatically, even amongst those made by the identical maker.

2. Engineer's square-- these are comparable in design to the try squares, however, made completely of steel. Blades lengths begin at roughly 2 in. These squares are more dependable as opposed to try squares, most likely since engineers are a more demanding lot than woodworkers. Engineer's squares could be utilized interchangeably with try squares.

3. Framing squares-- these are created for building a house. They have 2 big blades which constitute an appropriate angle. One blade is 2in broad by 24in long; the other is 1 1/2 in by 18in long. Framing squares are not counted on to be accurate as engineer's squares or try squares.

Marking Tools

1. Pencils-- each store requires pencils to mark your designs out and to mark wood so as to monitor jointed surfaces and which part fits together where.

2. Knives-- these are vital in a woodshop for activities like cutting cardboard templates and marking tenon shoulders. You have a choice with knives. Box cutters, pocket knives, utility knives with a retracting blade are all beneficial in a woodworking store.

3. Awls-- these are pointy, pointed tools with a range of functions. They vary in their point fineness and their shaft density. A fine-pointed awl works for scribing lines and marking out joinery, and a broad-pointed, thick-shanked awl is excellent for creating pilot holes in wood before drilling. The dimple it leaves when tapped with a mallet creates a precise beginning point for a drill part.

Chapter 5: Chisel Essentials.

There are just a couple of genuinely vital hand tools for woodworking these days. Close to the top of the list would be the standard chisel. This tool accomplishes it all, from thoroughly paring away thin shavings in elaborately comprehensive work to rapidly scooping out big pieces of wood waste. You are going to discover chisels in each standard element of woodworking from furniture creating to woodcarving to trim carpentry.

There are numerous various kinds and sizes of chisels one needs to carry in their woodworking shop and every one is created for a particular task. You might think about buying a 4 piece set that includes 1/4-, 1/2-, 3/4- and a 1-inch beveled bench chisel with blade lengths between 4 and 6 inches. Plastic handles are most effective since they are able to withstand being struck by a mallet and are comfy to wield for extended time periods. If you just have the budget for one, buy a 3/4 inch chisel and make sure to buy a dependable brand due to the fact that quality matters, it is going to hold up to repeated honing longer.

Utilizing Your Chisel

To notch at the edge of a bit of wood or to chisel a shallow mortise, start by positioning the indentation edge with a blade grove. And after that, position the beveled edge ahead of the throw-away place, place the edge of the chisel in the following line, holding the chisel perpendicularly and tap using your mallet that makes the cuts across the border. Put the bevel facing down; make one-sided cuts from the stock exterior to the boarder cuts to create the indentation walls. Following the angled border cuts to the wanted depth, turn the chisel bevel side up and slice diagonally versus the grain and eliminating most of the worthless parts. When the indentation has actually come to its determined measurement, utilize small cuts to assist with reaching its last depth and size .

Utilize a broad bevel chisel, with the bevel up in a sweeping, semi-circular movement with the straggling blade end performing the slicing, in case, you want engrain paring done.

The simplest and fastest method to slice a spacious mortis is to initially drill a series of holes using a drill bit which is somewhat smaller than the hole depth. After that, utilize the chisel to shear the disposable bits away amidst the holes.

Concave curves could be trimmed by utilizing a chisel in order to be relatively broader than the reserve width. Push down on the blade while turning down on the handle and pressing diretly ahead as you are holding down the bevel.

Sharpening

For quick and tidy cutting and, a sharpened edge is needed as well as for personal well-being. An tool that is not sharp makes a rough cut-- you wish for everything to be effortless-- yet the extra strength required to drive the tool might result in you having less control over the scenario which might cause accidents.

By sharpening a chisel routinely on a oil or water stone, you are going to maintain it sharp and in finest shape for scraping and cutting. The cutting edge bevel is usually about 20 to 35 degrees. Nevertheless, you do not need to sharpen the total bevel. In its place, sharpen a little, small bevel on top to a bit more of an angle than the most essential bevel.

Place the bevel on the stone firmly and after that rise the chisel around 5 degrees. Move the blade backward and forward up until an edge of a wire builds on the rear of the blade. Turn the blade over and place it completely on the stone, move it backward and forward a couple of times to remove the wire edge. Pare across an end grain as a test for irregularity.

Chapter 6: Selecting Hand Tools.

There are numerous woodworkers who think that utilizing hand tools and just hand tools is the method to create anything. From birdhouses to furniture, just hand tools are going to do for them. Others are going to utilize a mix of portable power tools and hand tools and possibly sedentary devices such as a table saw or other big machinery that aids to move the procedure along quicker.

Hand tools are silent and allow you to connect with the wood on a separate level by utilizing devices to cut or rip the wood. Here is a list of numerous hand tools you ought to have in the event that you find yourself wishing to end up being one with the wood.

Chisels-- always buy an excellent set of wooden-handled bench chisels (1/4 in, 3/4 in, 1in) and a 1/4 in mortise chisel. Wood handles are cozier and more aesthetically pleasing than plastic and in case they ever get damaged or split, you could substitute them with a bit of effort. Western chisels are more favored than the Japanese ones, which some say needs excessive work, specifically if you're simply beginning in woodworking. If you can pay for it, purchase a 2in broad bench chisel, along with the 4 tinier ones. Its extra-wide blade is perfect for tenon paring.

Sharpening stones-- Waterstones are more clean when compared to oilstones. They are available in a range of grits.

Combination square-- typically can be found in 12 in. This instrument is going to mark out stock at 45 and 90 degrees and could function as a marking gauge and a ruler. Purchase the best you are able to pay for due to the fact that you are going to be utilizing it the most.

Hammer-- a great 13-oz, a claw hammer is perfect for basic cabinet work and works for setup work too. They are affordable, yet do the job properly the initial time.

Caver's mallet-- this works for chopping out mortises and driving joints home. A medium-sized turned lignum vitae mallet is roughly $20-25.

Dovetail and tenon saws-- utilized for chopping little pieces, an 8in dovetail saw with 18 teeth per inch and a turned handle. A 10in brass-backed dovetail saw with 14 teeth per inch for chopping tenons and dovetails. Japanese saws are going to do an excellent job additionally; nevertheless, they can necessitate precise handling and replacement blades are typically costly.

Block plane-- block plane could either be a routine angle or a low-angle. They are strong, compact and properly crafted. A block plane works for planning little parts, planning end grain and flushing surfaces.

Smoothing plane # 3-- a smoothing plane is utilized for the last preparation of surfaces and also for faring joints and for shooting edges on short pieces. Count on paying upwards of $110 for something good.

Rabbet plane-- there are a number of planes that suit the bill, this plane is utilized to cut rabbets, trim joints and plane into corners. A few of them have a detachable front half to transform it into a chisel plane.

Spokeshaves-- this is a kind of plane utilized mostly to round edges, create spindles and reasonable concave curves. The short spokeshave sole is installed in between two handles. The blade is normally kept in place with a cap iron. They could be utilized with either pulling or pressing movement.

Cabinet scraper-- they are affordable, work properly and last for what appears like eternity. Scrapers are great for refining veneered and hardwood surfaces, either in lieu of sanding or before.

Burnishers-- these are smooth rods of tough steel utilized to place an edge on a scraper. They could be oval, round or triangular in section. An extremely refined burnisher generates a smooth scraper edge, which consequently makes the scraped wood smoother. The Phillips-head screwdriver shank frequently functions effectively as a burnisher.

Drill bits-- the drill bits discovered in a woodshop consist of brad-point bits, twist drills, Forstner bits and spade bits. Each has unique benefits and constraints.

Clamps-- there are a variety of clamps utilized to squeeze bits of wood together especially throughout gluing and assembly. Bar clamps are composed of 2 jaws mounted on a length of steel bar and I-shaped in section. A pipe clamp is comparable except that it replaces a pipe for the I-bar and is less rough. Pipe and bar clamps are ideally suited for assembling broad surfaces, like tabletops and for assembling big carcasses.

Chapter 7: Adhesives

Even though there are roughly 1,500 adhesive items made in the U.S., less than a dozen are appropriate for woodworking. Prior to entering into the individual adhesive kinds, it may be valuable to understand how the glue binds wooden parts together. It is valuable to comprehend a bit about the chemical makeup of wood and how an adhesive connects with these elements throughout the bonding procedure. Wood is an intricate mix of water and organic chemicals.

Roughly 95 percent of the board is composed of hemicelluloses, cellulose and lignin, which shape the wooden structural matrix and grant it its strength, durability and flexibility. The remaining 5 percent contained within dry wood is comprised of essential oils, tannins, gums, resins, sugars and coloring agents. This chemical blend of extractives causes wood's odor, color and decay resistance.

As soon as an adhesive is administered to surrounding wood surfaces and the bits are secured up, the structural aspects of the wood are connected together by the bonding procedure. Initially, the fluid adhesive is soaked up into the wood and its polymer particles come together with the structural wood fibers. Then, the adhesive's polymer particles merge or come together, encompass the structural fibers and solidify, interlocking the fibers mechanically.

Thermosetting glues like urea-formaldehyde, resorcinol and epoxy cure by a chemical reaction, typically after 2 elements have actually been combined, while thermoplastic adhesives, like white and yellow glues cure by evaporations. As soon as either kind of glue is dry, the cured adhesive thin layer in between the two wooden surfaces functions as a bridge keeping the boards together.

Polyvinyl Acetates

White and yellow glues are most likely the most frequently and most prominent glues utilized in woodworking these days. Both are polyvinyl acetates (PVA) adhesives that can be found in 3 primary varieties: craft or white glue, yellow aliphatic resin, and cross-linking PVA emulsion. All of these have a well-balanced set of characteristics, that make them perfect for gluing wood. They are simple to utilize, have a fast grab, aren't toxic and operate in many wood-gluing circumstances. Additionally, the liquid adhesives are going to spoil if frozen. Nevertheless, PVA adhesives have bad creep resistance and they must never ever be utilized in structural assemblies, such as load-bearing beams, without some type of mechanical securing like with screws or nails.

Resorcinol and Urea-Formaldehyde

Resorcinol formaldehyde adhesives and urea-formaldehyde are most often utilized for bonding wood when sturdy, creep- and waterproof bonds are needed. Urea-formaldehyde (UF) adhesive, in some cases, referred to as plastic resin glue comes as a one-part powder. The powder is a blend of dry hardeners and resins that if maintained dry are going to stay storable forever. Water is included to liquefy the chemicals and trigger the adhesive. The pot life after blending is fairly long. However, the activated glue viscosity gradually increases up until after approximately an hour, the adhesive is too dense to work with. When cured, UF adhesives create structural bonds and the tan glueline is barely visible even on light-colored woods. Hardwood plywood panels and interior load-bearing beams are frequently glued with UF adhesives. Nevertheless, it is not one hundred percent water-resistant.

Resorcinol formaldehyde have substantial strength, remarkable solvent resistance and when effectively cured are going to endure extended water immersion, making them ideal for marine applications. RF glues come as two-part sets: part one is the resorcinol resin liquified in ethyl alcohol; the other part consists of powdered paraformaldehyde. The premeasured parts are whisked together to set off the adhesive, however mindful blending is required to prevent lumps.

Dealing with UF and RF adhesives can trigger health problems, so operate in a well-ventilated location, use a mask and take breaks when possible. This is since they both release formaldehyde gas.

Epoxy

With their substantial strength, fantastic gap-filling capability, capability to structurally join difficult-to-bond components and water-resistant nature, epoxies are undoubtedly the high-performance adhesives of the woodworking realm. Epoxy includes an amine hardener and epoxy resin. Generally, equivalent parts of hardener and resin are combined to set off the adhesive and begin the curing procedure, which functions by chemical reaction instead of solvent evaporation. The precise blending percentages are pretty crucial; too much of either element is going to negatively impact bonding strength. Due to the absence of solvent, epoxy has a remarkable gap-filling capability.

Chapter 8: Sharpening Tools

There are a number of methods to keep your woodworking tool sharp. Many are kept sharp by utilizing an abrasive whetstone to wear the metal to a slim cutting edge. The better-quality natural stones are more costly, however you can get satisfying arise from less expensive, artificial stones. As aspect of the sharpening, whetstones are lubricated with oils or water to ensure the steel does not get too hot and to stop fine particles of stone and metal from obstructing the abrasive surface.

Typically, whetstones are offered as rectangular blocks-- called bench stones-- for sharpening regular tools or as little knife edges or teardrop section stones for sharpening gouges and etching chisels. Blades could additionally be sharpened on a completely flat metal plate which has actually been cleaned with abrasive powder.

Oilstones

Most of manufactured and natural sharpening stones are lubricated with light oil. Novaculite, typically considered to be the best oilstones out there, are just discovered in Arkansas. This compact silica crystal occurs naturally in different grades. The course, mottled-gray Soft Arkansas stone gets rid of metal rapidly and is utilized for the initial edged tool shaping. The white Hard Arkansas stone places the sharpening angle on the cutting edge, which is then fine-tuned and refined using the Black Arkansas stone. Even finer is the uncommon translucent variety. Artificial oilstones are created from sintered silicon carbide or aluminum oxide. Classified as medium, coarse and fine, manufactured sharpening stones are far more affordable than their natural equals.

Waterstones

Since it is reasonably soft and crumbly, a sharpening stone which is lubricated with water cuts quicker than a comparable oilstone; fresh abrasive particles are exposed and discharged continuously as a meta blade is rubbed over the waterstone surface. Nevertheless, this soft bond additionally makes a waterstone susceptible to unintentional damage, particularly when sharpening narrow chisels that might score the surface. Naturally occurring waterstones are so pricey that the majority of tool providers provide just the synthetic varieties that are almost as effective.

Diamond Stones

Very resilient coarse-- and fine-grade sharpening 'stones' consist of a nickel-plated steel plate which is implanted with monocrystalline diamond particles and bound to a rigid polycarbonate foundation. These quick-cutting sharpening tools, offered as narrow files and bench stones, could be utilized lubricated with water or dry. Diamond stones are going to sharpen carbide and steel tools.

Metal Lapping Plates

Offered as alternatives to standard sharpening stones, oiled steel or cast-iron plates sprayed with successively finer silicon carbide particles create a definitely flat polished back to a plane or chisel blade and razor-sharp cutting edges. For the supreme cutting edge on steel tools, end with diamond-grit substance spread on a flat steel plate. Diamond abrasives are additionally utilized to sharpen carbide-tipped instruments.

Chapter 9: Making Joints

Square-Ended Butt Joints

It is attainable to create flat frames and straightforward box structures using square-cut corner joints. Utilize sawn wood for rough woodworking, but plane the wood square ahead of time for high-quality cabinet work. Because glue alone is hardly ever sufficient to create a durable butt join, keep the parts together with glued wooden blocks or fine nails.

Mitered Butt Joint

The traditional picture frame joint, the mitered butt joint makes a cool right-angle corner with no noticeable end grain. Cutting wood at 45 degrees creates a reasonably big surface area of weight frames. Only include glue and set the join in a miter clamp for some time.

Edge-to-Edge Butt Joint

Lumber choice is essential as excellent edge-to-edge joints when creating a broad panel from strong wood. To make certain the panel is going to stay flat; attempt to utilize quarter-sawn wood-- that is, with the end-grain growth rings going perpendicular to the face side of every board. In case that is not feasible, set them up so the orientation of ring growth shifts from one board to another. Additionally attempt to ensure the board surface grain runs in an identical direction, to assist with the last panel cleaning up with a plane. Prior to getting started with work, number every board and mark the face sides.

Tongue and Groove Joint

Utilize a combination plane to chop a tongue-and-groove joint manually. This type of plane resembles a common plow plane. However, it features a broader variety of cutters, consisting of one developed to form a tongue on the workpiece edge. Cut the tongue initially, then alter the cutter and plane a matching groove.

Doweled Frame Joints

Frames created with dowelled butt joints are remarkably sturdy. These days, the majority of factory-made furniture integrate dowel joints even for chair rails, which need to be capable of withstanding extended and substantial stress. Most of the times, 2 dowels per joint suffice. Put them a minimum of 1/4 inch from both sides of the rail.

Edge-to-Edge Dowel Joint

When building a broad solid-wood panel, you are able to create an especially sturdy join between boards by placing a dowel every 9 to 12 inches.

Carcass Butt Joints

When building a carcass with butt joints which are bolstered with several dowels, it pays to purchase extra-long slide rods and extra drill bit guides for the doweling jig. A doweling jig is needed for a number of the dowelled joints. This could be a pricey piece of equipment and in case you are not going to utilize it really frequently, it may be worth considering borrowing or leasing one.

Corner Bridle Joint

A corner bridle joint is sufficient for fairly lightweight frames, as long as they are not exposed to sideways pressure, which has a tendency to push bridle joints out of square. The power of the bridle is boosted substantially in case you insert 2 dowels through the joint edge after the setting of the glue.

Mitered Bridle Joint

The mitered bridle is cut in a comparable fashion as the traditional corner joint, yet it is a more appealing option for framing, since end grain shows up on a single edge only.

T-Bridle Joint

The T-bridle joint functions as an intermediate support for a frame and with adjustments, is often utilized to join a table leg to the underframe when a long rail needs support. Unlike the corner bridle, which is fairly weak under sideways pressure, the t-bridle is comparable in durability to the mortise-and-tenon joint.

Lap Joint

A standard lap joint is just partially more powerful than a simple butt joint, however, it is an improvement in look given that the majority of the end grain is hidden. Consequently, it is, in some cases, utilized as a fairly basic method of linking a drawer front to drawer sides.

Through Mortise and Tenon Joint

The through joint, where the tenon goes straight thought the leg, is utilized a lot for construction frames of all varieties. With the end grain showing, perhaps with wood wedges utilized to disperse the tenon, it is an appealing professional joint. Constantly cut the mortise initially, because it is simpler to make the tenon fit precisely instead of the other way around.

Chapter 10: Choosing What To Construct

The initial step of any woodworking undertaking involves preparation. A straightforward project might take simply a little bit of planning before you're prepared to build, however more complex furniture typically takes a lot more preparation. In either case, certain degree of preparation is important.

Project preparation has 3 standard phases: identifying what to build, figuring out the details via prototypes and illustrations, then determining components and cutting lists from your drawings.

Perhaps your family has actually outgrown the kitchen table and you wish to substitute it with something a bit uncommon. You could create any table you desire and personalize it to fit your individual requirements or tastes. Perhaps you have actually had your eye on an Arts and Crafts sideboard at the local furniture gallery, however, it's priced outside your means.

Creating one yourself enables you to manage the quality and expense. Perhaps you simply wish to try some brand-new woodworking methods or tools to broaden your skill base. The inspiration to construct something has a variety of sources.

Gathering ideas-- whatever your inspiration might be for constructing something, odds are you have actually already thought about it sufficiently to have some first ideas about layout. The idea-gathering phase is a crucial one. It's time to let your creativity go without devoting to any idea. Feed your ideas with a great deal of concrete choices so you are able to begin to define a design.

Furniture shops are fantastic locations to analyze various instances of different styles and kinds of furniture. Take a look at family and friends furniture, clip out pictures from magazines and brochures and have them in a idea folder of what you wish to construct.

Furniture follows certain classical design patterns and always has. Definitely, everything you create does not need to comply with an accepted design, however fundamental furniture style is the end outcome of centuries of experimentation. Examine proportions of tables, cabinetry, chests and chairs to get a feeling for how furniture works in conjunction with the body.

You'll understand a comfy chair when you sit in one, even though you can't determine why it feels so supportive. Seat size, height of the leg and the angle of the back-rest are all aspects that add to coziness.

Assess your abilities, instruments and budget-- maintain your skill level in mind as you examine the furniture. Furniture with relief carvings, delicate inlays or elements which joins at curves or angles are going to be harder to construct than pieces with direct lines and minimal decoration. If you're simply getting started, think about attempting projects in the Arts and Crafts, Shaker and country designs. These are excellent choices for constructing durable furniture without requiring sophisticated woodworking abilities or a complete toolbox of equipment or instruments.

Attempt a brand-new method occasionally within the furniture design to keep each undertaking exciting. Your roster of abilities is going to grow gradually without endangering the success of an entire project.

Building prudently indicates working with a form of project budget plan in mind. When your pockets for a venture aren't deep, the dollars are going to go further by constructing with 3/4 inch lumber instead of thick pieces of exotic hardwood. It's generally correct that the bigger your project ends up being physically, the more it costs.

Sheet products are typically cheaper and you could stay away from the wood movement problems you'll deal with when developing panels made from strong wood. Keep in mind to include the expense of special hardware your project is going to require, like hinges, slides, drawer pulls and doorknobs. These products certainly contribute to the bottom line of what your project costs to construct.

Before starting a project, take a look around your workshop at the instruments you have. Do you have all the tools you are going to require for cutting out your project components, forming the edges, smoothing the part surfaces or putting togetherpanels? If your project components are curved and little, how are you going to securely cut the small curves?

A scroll saw is the most ideal instrument for this job. Are you going to require one or can you customize the layout or achieve the job another way? Think through the building phase of the venture and how you'll handle each machining action. Otherwise, you might wind up midway through the task and baffled over how to continue. If you can't complete the task without purchasing a brand-new tool, is your budget going to support the expense?

Chapter 11: Developing Working Drawings

This is where the fun starts! You get your initial glimpse at the project-to-be and you could figure out the bugs in the general appearance of the piece without worrying about the details. Move toward concept sketching by giving your hand 'unlimited freedom' to draw and redraw any ideas that enter your mind. This is not the time to stress over best proportion, appropriately scaled parts, sharp lines or exacting curves. You are able to take care of all that afterwards when you create the mechanical drawings. However, don't advance from sketching to drafting up until you have a thing you actually like. It's extremely time-consuming to make significant design adjustments at the drafting phase.

Select a soft #2 lead pencil, a pink-tipped eraser and an artist's sketchbook. Stay away from utilizing anything tougher since their lines are hard to remove from common sketch paper. Hold the pencil gently and simply move across the page up until anything comes to you. Enable your arm to move with your hand as you are making lengthy lines and rotate the sketch pad as you organically sweep your wrist all over the paper when drawing angled lines.

Among the advantages of doing 'freehand idea sketches' is that you could quickly develop a series of 'what-if' views. Rather than redrawing the form repeatedly, just trace it onto a piece of clear paper, excluding the locations that are going to be altered in the 'what-if' views. Or you are able to copy as many standard outlines as you 'd want and after that flesh them out with your brand-new idea.

As soon as you have actually decided on an idea, sketch what comes nearest to what your idea is. It's time to appoint some dimensions to the task. By laying out the design to scale in a mechanical drawing, you are able to see plainly how the shape and size of parts connect to each other. Techniques and series of joinery additionally end up being more apparent. These working illustrations are a bridge between your freehand idea illustrations and a master cut list.

Preparing Fundamentals

These abilities are primarily common sense: make certain your board is without eraser and lead particles prior to taping the paper to it. Line up the paper bottom to the parallel rule and after that attach it to the board with a bit of tape in every corner. Have a scrap piece of paper in between the drawing and your hand to prevent smearing your work. Utilize a brush to clean away eraser particles, not your hand. As soon as you develop a baseline on your sketch, draw any degree angle to it utilizing either a straightedge and a protractor or a angle design templates.

Start the angled line accurately on a dimension mark by holding the pencil to the mark and after that moving the straightedge or template to it. in case you reverse this procedure, parallax could delude your eyes, inducing you to misjudge the pencil positioning. Tilt the pencil a little into the corner created in between the design template edge and the paper to draw out a waver-free line..

A mechanical drawing is absolutely nothing more than a proper line meeting which show the layout of an item and where measurements are being made to. Unless these lines differ somehow, the illustration could be tough to read.

Chapter 12: Fillers and Finishes

There are numerous finishes, every one of which has weak and strong points. They differ in the simplicity of application, solvent resistance, water resistance, dirt resistance, sturdiness, surface accumulation toxicity, gloss and ease of repair. The most typically utilized finishes are varnishes and urethane, varnish/oil mixes, cleaning varnishes, wax, lacquers and shellac.

Oils

Two kinds of oil are utilized to finish furniture: linseed oil which is pushed from tung oil and flax seed which originates from the tung tree nut. Although tung oil came from China, a lot of it is now shipped from South America. Tung oil is better than linseed oil, with higher water resistance and less propensity to yellow gradually.

In their purest forms, these oils dry gradually and remain fairly soft. To make them dry harder and quicker, they are frequently treated with heat and/or ingredients in the production procedure. Treated linseed oil is referred to as 'boiled' linseed oil.

The benefits of oil finishes are:

Simplicity of application, you simply place a bit of oil on the wood with a rag, allow it soak in and erase the surplus.

Look--When effectively used, oil finishes dry in the wood, instead of on top of it. The lack of surface accumulation offers the wood a tactile and visual immediacy that many other finishes do not have.

Simplicity of repair, stains and scrapes could be re-oiled and sanded out without removing the whole surface. Nevertheless, on woods that alter color due to oxidation or direct exposure to sunshine, a newly sanded area is going to remain a different color for a long time.

The downsides of oil finishes are:

- Fairly little defense versus liquids, wetness and scratches.

- Numerous coats are needed to establish a good accumulation.

- Wet oil may bleed out of the pores for hours.

Urethane and Varnish

Varnishes are surface area coatings typically created by cooking resin and oil together and integrating the mix with thinner, mineral spirits. Contemporary varnishes generally replace artificial alkyd resin for natural resin. Urethane is really comparable to varnish, except that it consists of some percentage of polyurethane resin.

Varnish is used with a brush, dries much less easily than oil requires takes a long period of time to dry. Exceptional water solvent resistance and wetness, in addition to abrasion protection, makes varnish a perfect finish for marine and outside usages. Care and practice are needed in using varnish, which easily reveals brush marks, picks up particles of dirt and traps air bubbles.

Oil/Varnish Mixes

Oil/varnish mixes are used such as oil yet dry quicker and tougher with less coats needed to develop an attractive surface. There is no surface coating for ruining the wooden tactile quality. Even though they aren't nearly as preventive as dense straight varnish coats, oil/varnish mixes definably offer greater wetness and liquid protection than does oil by itself.

Drawbacks of oil/varnish mixes are biggest on tabletops since standing water permeates them. The outcomes could be staining of the finish and/or staining and alteration of wooden texture.

Wax

Waxes are typically utilized as a coating over other finishes, instead of as a main finish. It does not offer a lot of protection. However, it can considerably improve the look. Typical waxes utilized on furniture consist of paraffin, beeswax and carnauba. Many commercially offered paste-wax finishes consist of several of these waxes, blended with a solvent to make them sufficiently soft for simple application.

Wiping Varnishes

Much of the 'oil' and 'tung oil' items offered to woodworkers nowadays are, in fact, wiping varnishes-- varnishes that have actually been thinned with a high percentage of mineral spirits, even though certain 'tung oil' items do not include any tung oil. Wiping varnishes are used such as oil finishes, but are dry as slim surface coating. Given that many applications would be needed to develop an ample finish depth to enable the glossy surface to be rubbed out uniformly, a thin varnish coating has a tendency to appear streaky and inexpensive.

Shellac

Shellac is created from a lac beetle secretation. It came from the Orient and was long the premier finish for great European furniture, but has typically been substituted by more resilient artificial lacquers. Shellac is fragile, as are lacquer and varnish. The great crackling we link with antiques is shellac's reaction to the seasonal motion of wood. Shellac is additionally rapidly harmed by alcohol or water.

Lacquers

Lacquers describe a broad family of artificial finishes. These consist of the brand-new water-based lacquers and the more conventional nitrocellulose-based lacquers. Lacquer is typically used with spray guns and the so-called 'padding lacquer' is actually shellac. Just like shellac and varnish, lacquer is a surface finish.

Fillers

The open-grained wood pores like mahogany and oak have a tendency to telegraph through a surface finish, specifically in reflected light. Unless the pores are filled in advance, numerous finish layers need to be sanded flat and applied to fill them well before surface accumulation can start. Fillers are delicate powders or pastes that could be tinted to suit the wood.

They are utilized to fill open pores prior to using the finish. Typically, the Paris plaster was utilized to fill mahogany prior to French polishing. Now, paste filler which is created from silica that has actually been blended with a oil or varnish binder and thinned with naphtha.

I hope that you enjoyed reading through this book and that you have found it useful. If you want to share your thoughts on this book, you can do so by leaving a review on the Amazon page. Have a great rest of the day.

Printed in Great Britain
by Amazon